John Rutter

The Culture and Diseases of the Peach

A complete treatise for the use of peach growers and gardeners

John Rutter

The Culture and Diseases of the Peach
A complete treatise for the use of peach growers and gardeners

ISBN/EAN: 9783337068967

Printed in Europe, USA, Canada, Australia, Japan

Cover: Foto ©Lupo / pixelio.de

More available books at **www.hansebooks.com**

THE CULTURE AND DISEASES OF THE PEACH;

A COMPLETE TREATISE

FOR THE

USE OF PEACH GROWERS AND GARDENERS,

OF

PENNSYLVANIA,

AND ALL

DISTRICTS AFFECTED BY THE "YELLOWS,"

AND

OTHER DISEASES OF THE TREE.

BY JOHN RUTTER,

West Chester, Pa.

Ex-President of the Chester County Horticultural Society and Honorary Member of the Pennsylvania Fruit Growers' Society.

HARRISBURG, PA.:
EVERY SATURDAY NIGHT OFFICE.
1880.

Entered, according to act of Congress, in the year 1880, by
JOHN RUTTER,
in the Office of the Librarian of Congress at Washington.

INTRODUCTORY.

———:o:———

A desire to see the great State of Pennsylvania, and more especially its rich and fertile districts east of the mountains, engaged in the cultivation of the Peach, and supplying the markets of its cities with this luscious fruit, instead of spending thousands of dollars annually for the benefit of the peach growers of Delaware and Maryland, is the impulse that prompted me to write the following pages, and to present them to the public.

It is well known that the Peach would be extensively cultivated in this State, did not the fatal disease, the Yellows, prevent its successful cultivation. My long experience in the cultivation of this fruit gives me the passport to a correct knowledge of this disease, and how to prevent it. In these pages will be found the results of my experience, and the description of successful manipulation of the peach orchard to combat its diseases.

If these instructions are followed out by our farmers and fruit growers generally, the day is not far distant when Eastern Pennsylvania will supply the markets of Philadelphia and New York with better peaches than now come from the celebrated peach districts of Delaware and Maryland.

JOHN RUTTER.

West Chester, March 1, 1880.

THE PEACH AND ITS DISEASES.

---o---

IT is universally admitted that the Peach is regarded as the most delicious, popular, and highly esteemed of all the summer and fall fruits grown within the limits of our temperate climate and particularly within the Middle States. It was introduced by the early settlers of the country at different places and at different periods, from 1650 to 1680, taking rank with the apple and the small fruits around the rustic habitations, adding its rich tribute to the scanty luxuries of these heroic pioneers in our American forests. Keeping pace with the successive settlements of the country, by the hardy adventurers of almost every nation, it became indispensible to the garden and orchard—these Edens of their primitive homes. The tree grew in the newly upturned virgin soil of the country in great vigor and fruitfulness, from Massachusetts to the extreme settlements in the South, giving the most unmistakable evidence of its adaptability to the soil and climate of its new location, reveling for the time under the shelter and protection of the forests, and free from all insect depredations or injury from disease, and rivaling in growth and productiveness the famed orchards of Persia and China, the reputed countries of its birth.

Such is its great excellence from improved varieties now cultivated and known to the country, and as exposed in our markets daily through the season of its maturity, that we can scarcely be charged with undue enthusiasm in rating the superior qualities of the Peach—its lusciousness of taste and great beauty of color—by uniting in our praise with the old Pomologists "that it excels all other fruits of the earth." It has been aptly said that no fruit this side of Paradise has ever rivaled it, and as a wholesome fruit of the season it has the highest character from the medical profession. Half a century ago the expression was often quoted "that a basket of healthy ripe Peaches in the market was worth more than a pound of calomel in the shop, and that it robbed the doctor of a patient and the druggist of a prescription." In its adaptability to the soil and climate of the United States the Peach is assigned the widest range of any other fruit, and such is the estimation in which it is everywhere held, that even in countries beyond its climatic limits of open culture, it finds a place in the orchard house forced under glass or on the trellis against a southern wall, under the care and skill of the expert gardener, and is considered the greatest luxury of the season. So well is this fruit known throughout the country and especially in Pennsylvania, that it would be but a repetition of what we already know to go into any detail of its history, other than in connection with the injuries and diseases to which it is subject, and particularly as affecting us here in Pennsylvania, within reach of the markets of Philadelphia and New York. In this connection I use the words INJURIES and DISEASES, as it is generally believed that the peach tree is specially subject to injuries and diseases over and above all other varieties of fruit trees common to our gardens and orchards. In removing this delusion I am pleased to be able to say—that from my experience in the cultivation of this fruit in Pennsylvania, Delaware and Maryland, which has been quite extensive, and from my personal observations over a region extending from New York to Florida—which observations have neither been casual nor limited in all this range of a varied soil and climate—I have seen and learned of but one disease destructive to the tree, and that is the specific disease termed the "yellows," and one as fatal to the Peach as yellow fever is to the human race, calling for a specific remedy or preventative to arrest its progress. All other causes affecting the peach tree are but slightly injurious and of but little account, and are found prevailing as well in what is considered the healthy peach districts in Southern Maryland, and further south, where the tree now stands in thrifty growth and productiveness, having attained a size of from one to two feet and over in diameter, and an age of from fifty to one hundred years. The injuries caused by the Peach borer and small insects that infest the bark and the leaves are mythical in comparison with the "yellows," a disease from which it has been said none survive. The borer for a long time was considered the active agent in causing the yellows. This opinion however has been long since exploded. His sharp cutting mandibles are as clear of communicating disease as the clean steel of the sharp instrument that follows him with unerring fatality to his rather insecure quarters at the root of the tree. The borer has been long enough the scape goat for the true "murderer," and although he is a most audacious sneak thief to the peach orchard, he carries no contagion or infection with him in his depredations in supplying his wants and gratifying his appetite. He makes no effort to escape our vigilance, but is always found at the scene of his depredations, and is as easily captured in Pennsylvania as in the great peach centres in Delaware and Maryland, the fields of his greatest success. In healthy and unhealthy districts as well as in healthy and unhealthy trees the borer is found and no place escapes him. He has no East, no West, no North no South—he is the autocrat of his empire eating out the substance of his people.

We will here for the present knowing his haunts and how to counteract and prevent his depredations leave him and turn our attention to the greater evil which prevails in the Eastern, Western and Northern States, and see what the scientific detectives have done and are now doing to discover the cause of the great ravages he has made in the peach orchard.

In placing this enemy in the category of those diseases which have been and continue to be so defiant to the advances of scientific investigation, let us still apply a due portion of attention in this direction in our comparison of the ravages of diseases that are counterpart to this one in animal life; such for example, as the pleuro-pneumonia in cattle, trichina in pork, rot and scab in sheep, rabies in that intolerable nuisance the dog, pleurisy and the hundred diseases the horse is subject to, and all the complicated ills of the human system where so many malign causes are constantly at work, baffling ages of professional research, and out of it all there come to us only palliatives and seldom any specific cures as a grand result in discovery.

Our Pomological writers in succession for the last half century, have gravely informed us that the Peach tree is short-lived in the North—a fact of which we all have been fully aware under its treatment with only a few exceptions against the proverbial rule, and our memory fails to carry us back to a different state of affairs. In the South however we find the reverse; and such too was the case in the North, for a century and more, after the introduction of the Peach into this country, and even now in healthy districts it grows to an old age, retaining its thriftiness for fifty and a hundred years, thus virtually giving it the character of a longlived tree. These facts alone fully demonstrate that the *cause* producing the change to a dwarfed size and short life, has not arisen from any want of adaptability in soil and climate, but is occasioned by disease to which we shall presently more fully refer. In order to reach our present object—which is to show that peaches in Pennsylvania and in the Middle States *can* be grown in orchard culture, as a branch of farm industry with greater success and to more profit to the producer, than they are now raised in Maryland and Delaware, or indeed in any of the peach districts farther South under a system of proper culture, I may here say this has been done for years and fairly tested with the same careful culture as in the peach districts of Southern Maryland. In showing this state of facts we will first present the early records reaching back to the first appearance of the fatal disease, in as brief a manner as possible to be intelligent. To do this, we must trace its progress and the course of examinations which have been made looking to the cause and the results obtained therefrom.

It is said that this disease—the yellows—made its first appearance in the neighborhood of Philadelphia. As to the truth of this declaration, the evidence is not at all clear. The first public notice on the subject we find in a communication made by

Judge Richard Peters, President of the Philadelphia Agricultural Society, dated February 11, 1806, and published in the transactions of that Society—which was instituted in 1785. From this carefully prepared article, it is evident that the Judge took a deep interest in the growth and cultivation of the Peach. He states " I know not in the catalogue of our trees, one more desirable, nor one more subject to mortification, decay and disease than the Peach. I have cultivated it from my early youth—about fifty years ago on the farm on which I now reside, my father had large peach orchards which yielded abundantly and they so continued for years, producing plentiful crops with but little attention—then the trees began nearly at once to sicken and finally perish. I have often found sick trees to infect those in vigor near them by some morbid effluvia." In this communication, Judge Peters refers to a plantation of 700 to 800 trees of natural fruit, which he calls an *extensive* orchard, and planted by Mr. Edward Heston, (near Hestonville, West Philadelphia, and near what is known as the Centennial grounds) on rather flat clay land, and states "that Mr. Heston begins to suffer by the disease I call yellows." Following up his observations in the progress of this disease in Mr. Heston's orchard, in September, 1807, he writes, "as I predicted the yellows are seen making destructive ravages in Mr. Heston's peach plantation. I have lost a great proportion of my trees by the same malady. This year some of them were young and vigorous but we have had two successive rainy seasons, and I do not recollect ever to have seen more general destruction among peach trees through the whole of the country. It seems evident that excessive moisture is one if not the primary cause of this irresistible disease."

I may here remark that my observations fully confirm this statement that wet seasons do favor the production of disease. The summer of 1878 was a wet season at West Chester, Pa., and in the immediate neighborhood, and I observed that the yellows was more than usually destructive among peach trees that had been cultivated in the usual careless way, or rather not cultivated at all.

Again, in Nov. 1807, Judge Peters, commenting on a letter he had received from Dr. Tilton, of Wilmington, Delaware, says, "I still think that the disease so generally fatal (more so this year than any other in my memory,) called the yellows is atmospheric. I have always considered mildew and blight as originating in atmospheric taint, yet Sir Joseph Banks asserts that *parasitical fungi*, and others affirm, that insects are the causes. I believe with much deference to authority so respectable, that fungi originate and insects breed in morbid juices and extravasated sap *after the plant has become sickly.*"

In his day Sir Joseph Banks was one of the most astute and accomplished naturalists England pos sessed, and he had given his attention to the investigation of the injurious *parasite fungi* of the kingdom, and he likewise presented a learned report on the causes of blight, mildew and rust in grain, and the discoveries he then made have been fully confirmed by subsequent scientific investigation.—*Parasitic fungi* are a cause of injury and fina destruction to healthy vegetable matter, as much so as the depredations made by insects, and as to Judge Peters " atmospheric taint," being a cause, it is about as lucid as the opinions of some of the old vegetable Physiologists, in assigning *vitiated* and *extravasated* sap as the direct cause of disease. The question behind it all would be what caused the taint; and what caused the extravasation of the sap—the hearts blood of the vegetable system? In the first place it might have been from a floating parasite fungi spore, or an infusoria in the atmosphere, but in that case " tainted" atmosphere would be a misnomer; and in the second place various causes might be at work through infusoria or fungi to produce extravasated sap and obstruct the natural channels of circulation. Sir Joseph Banks was correct in his fungi theory, as was proven by his and other practical tests—a discovery conferring no doubt lasting advantages to the grain growing interests of the kingdom of Great Britain. The tree or the plant, to continue its growth and development requires a free and unobstructed circulation of pure sap, conveying the pabulum of life suitable to its taste and physical constitution.

Dr. Tilton, of Wilmington, Delaware, in his correspondence with Judge Peters, Nov. 6, 1807, wrote as follows, "the disease and early death of our Peach trees is a fertile source of observation, and that in all the diseases of the Peach I have examined, it appears to me that insects do the mischief. The curling of the leaf, the boring of the bark, the destruction of the root, the premature ripening of the fruit, all proceed from insects, and even the sickly appearance of the tree called yellows is attributed to insects by a late writer in our newspaper! In my jaunt in Maryland, I was attentive to the subject of your letter. I found that peach trees were generally long lived, healthy and bore well. In Edward Lloyd's garden, I observed some of the trees fifteen to eighteen inches in diameter and perfectly healthy."

From these publications it seems that the experiments by Peters, and others, in the application of supposed cures and remedies were applied empirically, and opinions were expressed based only on slight indications, and hence errors and failures were the result. These gentlemen and others connected with their learned society, standing then as they did the living finger posts, directing the course in which public sentiment and public action should travel, rather discouraged than otherwise, perseverance of investigation into the causes of the troubles in peach growing, by advising farmers to let hazardous cultivation be collateral and subordinate, and apply their main strength to other employment more certain and equally profitable; concluding that peach trees could not be profitably cultivated on an extensive scale in that part of the country, that a succession of Peaches might be kept up for domestic use by " planting a few trees every year," and thus a death blow was given to general peach growing on a large scale, and it has only since been encouraged by the direction to plant a few Peach trees about the garden and buildings, and this has been observed in Eastern Pennsylvania to the present day, as one of the oracular sayings of the savants of that period. This pretext for the encouragement of our lazy indulgences without further effort to master the difficulties that beset us, and giving our time and attention to other departments of farming requiring less thought—giving us less profit and more labor—is the legacy left us by these writers and in our farming interests we are consoled with the dangerous doctrine that in our economic and domestic prosperity many things within our capacity to acquire by our own industry on the farms are cheaper to buy than to raise, thereby reversing the old maxim " that a penny saved is a penny earned," and just here for the want of a little more brain, a little labor, and another step higher up the ladder of energy, Pennsylvania is not only handing over annually, pennies, but millions of gold to her next neighbors, Delaware and Maryland, for products which she has the ability to raise in her soil and under almost the same climate, with the advantage of closer proximity to the great marts of consumption. In three or four short years with a proper application of common industry to this branch of fruit growing, the counties of Delaware, Chester, Lancaster, Montgomery, Bucks and Berks, alone would be able to relieve us of our dependence on our neighbors in the supply of these luxuries at least, for which we now pay so dearly. In looking to a renewed energy and a more improved and enlightened home industry in this direction, the time is not distant when these counties will emerge from their present condition in peach growing, and instead of mourning yearly over a few straggling, yellow dying trees about the dwelling, we shall see the thrifty, blooming productive orchard, adding its golden fruit to swell the profits of the farm, and contributing to the luxuries and comforts of home. The Peach now so shamefully neglected is not a new fruit to Pennsylvania, and the tree is no stranger to our productive soil and genial climate. It has been a servant and a good one, responding faithfully to our domestic culture for the last two hundred years wherever cared for, cultivated and protected, and often under our disgraceful neglect its energies and fruitfulness have only yielded to the visitation of a fell disease which it was our duty as well as our interest to endeavor to counteract, as we would the diseases in our faithful animals dependent upon us for support and protection, in return for a short life of labor in our fields. Let us in this strain turn to our Bibles, and learn again the price of good fruit at the Creation, as fixed by the Deity himself, and despair not. The injunction we there find is, "dress the garden and keep it." Can any one expect to obtain such a luxury as the Peach at a less price? In looking over that portion of the district of Eastern Pennsylvania, extending from the mountains to the Delaware river, we find but few who have regarded this injunction, while all others have rather followed the advice of Judge Peters, "to plant a few trees every year," and we have in this way kept up a kind of diseased perpetuity in the few yellow skeletons which have ornamented our habitations and surroundings for almost the past century. Let every farmer who has his own broad acres to cultivate, and every house keeper who has his garden to till, no matter how limited, read their own rebuke; not only in their diseased and sickly trees, but in the crowded markets of their own city, teeming in season with this delicious product which their industry should have supplied; and take wisdom for the future. We might here also awaken our languid interests by reading the parable of the vineyard, wherein idleness is called to industry, in the question, "Why stand ye here all the day idle?" It is quite evident that in Chester county, and it may be so in the adjoining counties, to which we have referred, that peach growing has increased but little in the past twenty years, and that from all the information we have obtained we have not advanced until lately, towards a settlement of the cause of the fell disease. In coming down to a more recent date we find that it is the old story repeated, and like all other ills and diseases, it keeps pace with the spread and extended settlement of the country. In every direction except toward the South, where its ravages have never extended, do we hear of its destructive influences. Many of the Western States, and especially those bordering on the region of the great lakes, as, for example, Wisconsin and Michigan, have gone extensively into peach growing for the purpose of supplying the markets of Chicago, and the other cities and towns of the great Northwest, and all complain of the ravages of the "yellows." The Legislature of Michigan has given the peach growers an act to prevent the spread of the disease, compelling the eradication of all trees from the orchard, when they present the first appearance of disease. This plan of ridding the orchards of diseased trees, cuts off its spread by contagion, which, as a rule, passes so rapidly over an orchard to the destruction of the healthy trees, and is one of the means for retarding its progress. This species of legislation is similar to that we have here in Pennsylvania, to prevent the spread of noxious weeds by enforcing the destruction of the plant before it matures its seed, the one plan removing the source of complaint through the destruction of the seed, and the other attaining the same object, if fungi is the cause of the spread of the disease. Some of our leading pomologists have from time to time, indulged in the notion that the "yellows" has had its day, and as late as the year 1873, one of the most prominent, in an address, informed us "that he was happy to say that the "yellows" is almost a thing of the past, and in many sections of our State (Pennsylvania), where the scourge held undisputed sway but a few short years ago, to-day can be seen healthy, thriving orchards, and consequently annual crops of delicious fruit. What is there in the season just passed to make it a marked epoch in the history of fruit culture? Is it not owing in a great measure to the peculiar temperature and possible lack of humidity in the atmosphere?"

These apparent cessations and almost entire disappearance of the disease in certain districts, for short periods of dry seasons are but mere temporary lulls in the ravages of the disease from suspended infectious malaria, inspiring the hope that in a short time it would become one of the "things of the past," but a returning season or two of favorable influences for the propagation of the disease, and all hope is dispelled by its renewed virulence. These appearances were noted in 1807, by that noted fruit grower—especially of the Peach—to whom I have already referred, Judge Peters, of

Philadelphia, and in a postscript to his letter we find the following: "We have had two successive rainy seasons, and I do not recollect ever to have seen more general destruction among peach trees through the whole of the country. It seems that excessive moisture is one, if not the primary cause, of this irresistible disease."

These coincidences of rainy seasons and the yellows among peach trees over the country, I have observed for years as marked in these alternations of weather, favoring the now general opinion of the cause of the disease as I have already remarked. Thomas Taylor, the microscopist of the Agricultural Department, Washington City, as published in the Agricultural Report of the year 1872, page 169, makes the following statement, "since contact with water dissolves this form of Næmosporo, viz: "Parasitic Fungi," without destroying the life of the spores, it is evident that the action of rain or washes of pure water will only tend to diffuse the spores over the body of the tree and roots, while the application of solutions of sulphuric acid and alkalies will destroy them."

There are strong confirmatory facts favoring the theory of "Fungi" as being the cause of disease, and that alkaline substances, such as caustic lime and potash are the proper substances as curatives for the disease, and with necessary precaution in the application of caustic lime, the destruction of the diseased agent is effected in a cheap and expeditious way, or the same end is accomplished in the application of ashes to the entire surface of the orchard. The trees introduced from the nursery, already diseased, when such disease shall appear, should be wed out and replaced by healthy young trees, first renovating the soil with an application of caustic lime, potash, or other strong alkaline substances.

My main object here is to satisfy the agricultural interests of Pennsylvania that peaches can be grown in the State on a scale commensurate with the demands of our cities and towns, in orchard culture, in larger quantities than they are now or can be raised in the most favored districts of Delaware or Maryland, and can be sent into our markets in better condition and at a much larger profit. As this is a declaration so entirely in conflict with the opinions of our people in Eastern Pennsylvania, I feel myself called upon to sustain the assertion in a very practical way, showing that what has been done for years can be done again throughout this and other States, all things being equal, and the recommendations here strictly observed—recommendations based on practical experience in peach culture for thirty-five years, in what is called the diseased peach district in Pennsylvania, and in the healthy districts on the Eastern shore of Maryland, cultivating and planting within that period from 25,000 to 30,000 trees; also an earlier experience in raising peaches in the State of Delaware, but on a smaller scale. And I may here repeat, that the accumulated evidence of all this period is fully and most overwhelmingly confirmatory of the declaration with which I set out. I was brought up from early boyhood in the apple and peach orchards of Delaware, and took my first lessons in grafting from an old almanac, and a knowledge of inoculating trees under the instruction of a good old neighboring Methodist exhorter.

Through these instrumentalities I became something of a pomologist of that early day—of a large country and small towns—and acquired a neighborhood reputation in the profession, but in a short time domestic changes took place, and I was called to other employments, carrying with me into Pennsylvania my taste and love for fruit culture, and particularly for my early favorite fruit, the Peach.

Some years after my location in West Chester, Pa., I made purchase of a farm on the "Mica Slate Ridge," some two and one-half miles north of the town. This ridge was known as the "Barrens," and the purchase was what, at this day, would be called a worn out-farm, but it was what I considered a miserably neglected one. Most of the farm land was out in "commons," and a range for road stock, under a crop of briars, and poverty grass.

The prospect was gloomy enough for making out of it anything by ordinary farming, unless by a heavy out-lay in fertilizers, and the aid of a doubtful tenant. It occurred to me, as it was near West

Chester, then a fair market even for foreign peaches, upon which we were depending, that it would be the best scheme for me to plant this land in peach trees, which, if successful, would give me a double advantage; first, by improving the land, and giving a crop of fruit for the market. In a proper routine of peach culture yearly, poor or medium land greatly improves; plowing down the weeds and stuff that springs up in the summer, with the foliage of the trees in the fall, is almost equal to a light coat of manure. Having fully determined on this course, against the ridicule of some and the remonstrance of other friends, with the old stereotyped declaration. "You can't raise peaches in Chester county," backed up by directing my attention to the hundreds of skeleton trees, dead and dying, about the yards and gardens of the town, and around the dwellings of the neighborhood, I went to work. All this was no terror to me, as I had seen it all in my younger days, in Upper Delaware, and I had enquired into the cause of it. If you want healthy peaches, do not plant your trees about a farm house, or in a farm garden, if it is an old one, unless you know of a proper system of renovation; for peach trees have been planted there from time immemorial, and in planting young trees, as many do every year or two, and on the very graves of a dozen predecessors, all of whom have died in rapid succession with the yellows, leaving the ground filled with the seeds of the disease, to seize on its new victim, is in effect courting failure. Indeed, even about modern houses, where but few trees have been planted, in nine cases out of ten, where a new tree is introduced, you will find two or three in the neighborhood perhaps in the last stages of disease, and through their poisonous contagion, or sporadic infection, if left in the ground, they will inoculate your young trees with disease the first season. To renovate the soil we must use caustic or quick lime, wood ashes, guano, poudrette or other alkalies, in sufficient quantity to destroy or neutralize the active agent in the soil, ready at all times to commit its ravages on the young trees —its natural food—and with this precaution, all trees affected by the yellows, which, from my description under the proper heading, may be recognized, must be removed, body and branch, and the earth renovated before replacing it with a young tree. In rejecting all the kind counsels of my friends, and feeling that I could bear the jocular remarks of others, I set myself to work, taking up everything that I could get my hands on, touching the subject of the disease of the tree, the only thing that could interfere to prevent my success. From my schooling in the orchard, in boyhood, knowing the routine of peach growing, in a rough way, having occasionally visited the mammoth orchards at Delaware city, and below, I had but one point in the whole field of peach growing to examine, and that was to find a preventative, or at least a palliative for the yellows. The peach borer, the curled leaf, and other things, in their feeble efforts, were mere *myths* compared with this one fatal scourge. In the course of my examinations, I found much good common sense and a good deal of nonsense on the subject, and as a specimen of the latter, I here give one or two little extracts, as they are from the brain of a Professor of Agriculture, Horticulture and Botany, in 1819: "There is but one stock proper whereon to bud peaches, which is the muscle plum, all other stocks are attacked by the *gum*, and by different species of *insects*, in particular the grub, an hexipode magot, which gets in between the cortex and the albumen, and prevents the sap from circulating, and produces what is commonly called the yellows."

"If the trees are injured with *mildew*, dip the branches infected in the liquid and it will immediately destroy the *insect*."

"If your orchards are troubled with mole hills, strew branches of elder about the ground, and they will soon disappear." "If you are troubled with snakes, plant ash around your orchard."

The most sensible articles I met with were the various letters and papers of Judge Peters, and correspondence gathering facts in relation to the disease, and particularly his reference to the investigations of Sir Joseph Banks, in his inquiries into the cause of blight, mildew and rust, which he found to be the result of parasitic fungi, and by fair analogy, the Judge considered it in connection with his inquiry into the cause of the yellows, but he differed with Sir Joseph in his correct conclusions, that fungi was the cause of the disease, and not the effect, and produced disease in healthy living vegetable matter. These conclusions, it seems to me, leave no room for doubt. Knowing that moss, lichens, fungi and vegetable matter were destroyed by caustic lime and potash, I concluded that a good coat of caustic lime, which was less expensive than ashes, could do no harm to the trees, at least if it did no good. So I ordered fifty bushels to the acre for twenty acres, but fortunately, through some mistake, seventy-five bushels to the acre were sent, and it was all spread, the land being first broken up deep, and well harrowed, and the lime, after spreading, harrowed in. The rows were struck eighteen by eighteen feet apart, of the depth of the original plowing; this, at the intersection of the cross-checking, made a place for each tree, only wanting a little levelling of the earth to receive them. One thousand trees were planted in the best part of the plot—if there was any best part to it. The ground in peaches was planted in corn, and the balance of the field sown down in oats and clover, and the corn, after the last dressing in the peach lot, was also sown down with clover. The following spring all the field was plowed down, and the balance planted with peach trees, with other lands, making up 5,000 trees, and all the land constituting the twenty acre field was planted in corn, manured in the hill with ashes, yard scrapings, &c., gathered about the barn. The other field, receiving the balance of the 4,000 trees, planted that spring, was treated as above described, except that the lime was reduced to fifty bushels per acre. After the second year the cropping was suspended in the first twenty acres, but the most of the other grounds were cropped for three years, in various crops, but mostly with corn, and after this was discontinued, the ground received one plowing and harrowing each year thereafter. The ground was generally plowed in the fall, harrowing mostly in the spring, and there was but little falling off in the crops of corn, in the second year, but in the third there was quite a reduction, as by that time the roots of the trees had quite covered the ground, interfering with the crop of corn. All of these trees made a rapid growth, and the first thousand bore a heavy crop the fourth year from planting, the fruit as fine as I ever raised before or since. I continued adding yearly to the orchards up to some 8,000 trees; this included an orchard in Delaware county, Pa., occupying a high piece of land of loamy soil, of strong Gneiss formation and and in fine condition. A strong grass sod was turned down, and the trees cropped in corn, for three successive years, and treated as the Chester county orchards, except in the question of liming, which was postponed for the want of time at planting, and was not put on till the following spring. All these orchards came into bearing condition the fourth season, bearing fine crops, except those coming in on unfavorable seasons, from late frosts. Sometimes the third season, if favorable, the young trees would make a light show of fine fruit. These orchards continued to produce well from twelve to fifteen years, glutting the West Chester market with the finest quality of fruit, and driving out all foreign supply for years; returning to my astonished friends, for their advice so kindly given, and as kindly rejected, the most substantial evidence of my entire success, establishing the fact, beyond a doubt, that peaches can be raised in Chester and Delaware counties at least, and on a large scale, and at an immense profit to the producer. These orchards more than paid the original cost of the land, on each bearing year, on a full or even half a crop. One season, of a very heavy crop, I rented out twenty acres I had some two miles from my general orchards, for $850. I had, at that time, some seventy acres in bearing, and the balance marketed, more than paid the original cost of the land upon which they stood.

IN turning to what, under more favorable circumstances than the preceding, just detailed, would be called "the dark side of the picture," I proceed to a recital of the difficulties encountered in the course of our management of the orchards referred to. I am most happy to say that the greatest, and the only one that caused the most anxiety, and for which I received the most condolence, arose from the trouble of disposing of my large crops of peaches, without glutting the surrounding markets, to the reduction of generous prices. Domestic markets pay better than those more distant, and particularly in cities, where competition is found in inferior fruit; but I console myself that in all these gluts, and excesses beyond demand, I had my reward in the removal of the old notion that Eastern Pennsylvania was not adapted to peach growing. From some cause or other that old scourge, the "yellows," was not so formidable an enemy as I had expected to have met, considering the remonstrances and persistent advice which my friends and neighbors had volunteered, and although this advice, so often rejected, may have had its impression, in the truthfulness of the adage, "that to be forewarned is to be forearmed," and that in these repeated forewarnings I had forearmed myself with the requisite instruments to successfully repel the assaults of the enemy, and to this we are, in an indirect way, indebted for the lights and shadows on the reversed side of this picture. The trees planted in the orchard were principally obtained from two or three New Jersey nurseries; one lot of which came from the interior of the State, and of a variety now common to our orchards, and of first quality in size and beauty—the Crawfords Late—and was grown in a well conducted nursery, but in a badly diseased district. I was informed by the nurseryman himself that the infection of the disease was so great, through the neighborhood, that he could scarcely raise sufficient for home use. At the same time, and for years before, he had been raising and inoculating nursery trees, and disposing of them largely to the peach growers in Delaware, Maryland, and elsewhere every year. This small lot of trees—not over 500, perhaps—gave me for several seasons more close inspection in detecting and weeding out diseased trees than all the rest of the orchards I possessed. I entertain no doubt, whatever, that the large percentage—which was not less than one-third to one-half of the trees—became diseased in the nursery, from a general infection, or in budding, trimming, or from some other local cause. I watched them closely, and on the first symptoms of the disease, as it appeared, the tree was removed, "root and branch," *at once*, to prevent any spread from contagion. I may remark, just here, and and most *emphatically*, that "*at once*" is the time to be observed in the removal of the diseased tree —suffering no delay to ripen up the approaching promising crop—and on the appearance of but a single specimen of *immature fruit* eradicate the whole tree; manifesting no sympathy, nor itching palm, to be relieved by a gold dollar or two in prospect of the crop; and no penny-wise and pound-foolish system of economy to be indulged in; but strike at once at the root of the evil, and save yourself, from, perhaps, a tenfold sacrifice.

Returning to the subject of the diseased lot of trees, spoken of above, in the course of a couple of years the disease ceased, and the balance remained healthy, requiring no further attention than the ordinary culture, and so continued, producing heavy crops, in years of bearing, with the rest of the orchard. The strongest evidence that this lot of trees became diseased in the nursery was the fact, that the rest of this orchard, and the others, planted mostly with trees from entirely a different section, exhibited no such appearance of disease, but only occasionally, here and there, one or two over a field of some twenty or twenty-five acres, continuing thus for perhaps some two or three years, but altogether outside of the lot of diseased trees above referred to. I do not think that I lost at any time in a series of years, over three per cent. by diseased trees, and this, we can readily count upon, as diseased trees from the nursery, not only from New Jersey and Pennsylvania, but from all nurseries in badly diseased districts. Assuming that fungi is the cause of "yellows," of which I think there is no doubt, and what we call diseased infections, spread by contact, budding, trimming, or in any other way, and as it affects the roots, body and limbs, any remedial agent, or any curative agent cannot at once, or in a year, surrounded as we may be by careless cultivators at times, whose only use is to cultivate parasitic fungi, and not peaches, prove effectual. In addition to this, we have to contend with that which I have just referred to, say one or two per cent., and for a time, perhaps more, of diseased trees from the nursery, and this we have to fight. In this aspect of the case, in addition to lime, potash, guano, poudrett, or other caustic alkalies, it will require the vigilant eye of the peach grower to detect the "exceptionals," that may so provokingly find their way into the orchard, and to nip them in the bud. The parasitic fungi that works the injury is microscopic, and not visible to the ordinary sight, and its seed or spore is its infection, and its touch is its contagion. A knife inserted through the bark of a diseased tree to the ever-moving current of sap may carry with it, in its incision into a healthy tree, a thousand spores, marking, in this way, their new victim to an early grave. This active sporadic agent appears on the body, branches and roots of the tree, and the application of alkalies, in a diluted state, may be made use of as a wash against their further spread. Caustic alkalies will destroy fungi—of this there can be no question. The peach grower, commencing right at the beginning of his work, can have no trouble, if he looks through his orchard several times through the season, and attends to these "exceptional" intruders, which have come uninvited from the nursery, or on a sporadic visit from a neighbor, and have all such as they appear rooted out, replanting other young trees in their place, and renovating the earth well with any caustic alkali, as ashes, guano, poudrett, &c.

It must be remembered that these experiments have not been confined to a dozen trees in an old garden, but extended to thousands, in open field culture, and not with one orchard, but with half a dozen, and not only in one location, but in several; one distant ten miles from the other, and in an adjoining county, and in a different formation of soil, and not planted at one time, but at different times. These orchards, during their bearing, for twelve to fifteen years, were noticed for their thrifty growth, health and productiveness, and as an evidence of it, an extensive nurseryman in Delaware, who raised large quantities of inoculated trees for sale every season, obtained his buds from these orchards, to keep his fruit trees for the market correct as to variety, and as a protection from the yellows, in taking buds from known healthy trees. The usual course among nurserymen is to cut their buds for inoculation from the nursery rows of the previous year's growth. As an introduction to another field of operation in peach culture, in a different soil and in a different climate, embracing a portion of the healthy peach districts of the State of Maryland, I may say that the Delaware railroad, connecting north with the Philadelphia, Wilmington and Baltimore railroad, a mile or two south of Wilmington, Delaware, with lateral branches, known to be the great avenues of trade and travel through almost the entire length and breadth of the peninsula, embraces the great peach regions of Delaware and Maryland. This road terminated, until after the close of the war, at Salisbury, Delaware, and at that time the peach and fruit district did not extend in that direction many miles below this point, for the want of facilities of transportation to the northern markets.

In 1864–5 the attention of our northern people began to be drawn in that direction, and particularly in and around the peach growing centres, some dropping below the terminus, in the direction of the proposed extended route of the railroad, where a pleasant, equable and healthy climate prevailed, having on the one side the Atlantic ocean, and on the other the Chesapeake Bay, equal of itself to an inland sea. The country is in every way adapted to early trucking and fruit growing, for the northern cities of New York and Philadelphia. Here fruits and vegetables mature some three weeks in advance of New Jersey and Pennsylvania, affording the producer the advantage of an early market and highly remunerative prices. I visited that section of country in July, 1865, and found the early peaches just ripening, and coming into market. This was about the twentieth of the month. These early shipments were then bringing high prices in Philadelphia and New York, and I was so pleased with the appearances that I contracted for the purchase of a farm, near the railroad, with a view of going into general fruit raising. This was in Somerset county, Maryland, some fifteen miles below the terminus, at Salisbury. A short time after the road was extended to Crisfield, on the bay. In the fall of 1865 and the spring of 1866 I commenced planting, putting in some 9,000 peach trees, and about twenty acres in pears, strawberries and grape vines. This section of Maryland was and is entirely exempt from the yellows. The disease, in fact, is not there known to peach growers. The extension of the railroad through to the bay induced the extensive planting of orchards, and the success attending my experiment with strawberries at once established that branch of fruit culture as highly profitable, and from less than one hundred quarts daily shipped from the station at the time I purchased, the shipments increased in two years to some 25,000 or 30,000 quarts per day, from the same station.

The peach tree there located, having no enemy to contend with but the borer, the caustic lime was not applied at planting, or at any other time. The trees were put in ordinary ground, without any fertilizer, and with good culture produced fine crops of peaches, commencing to bear the *third* year after planting. The early fruit brought fine prices in the northern cities, but the later peaches coming into competition with an overstocked market, from upper Delaware and Maryland, reduced the prices to such a low figure that often the expenses for baskets, collecting the fruit, freights, cartage and commissions consumed the whole price obtained, and, in fact, some consignments placed the consignee on the debtor side of the account, and the early profits were partly absorbed in the later shipments. To all this there is another serious drawback to peach growing in the South; for, as we proceed from Pennsylvania southward, even to Florida, the more precarious is the peach crop, from early blooming, succeeded by heavy frosts, and such is my experience in raising peaches North and South, that I am fully warranted in saying that the difference in this respect between West Chester, Pa., and Somerset county, Md., a distance of about one hundred and fifty miles, in a due line from North to South—taking a consecutive number of years, has been fully fifty per cent. of an increase in quantity in favor of West Chester, and in profits there is no approximate comparison. In Chester county the peach crops were more valuable than any other farm crops I ever raised, except my early strawberry crops in Maryland, while the peach crops in Maryland were quite unsatisfactory and discouraging from the causes assigned. The peach is a perishable fruit, and to enjoy it to the full, its rich, luscious saccharine taste, which it can only acquire at maturity on the tree, it must have a home market, a quick and careful conveyance, and then all these advantages can be enjoyed by the consumers in our cities and towns by its culture in the adjoining counties of Eastern Pennsylvania supplying the demand, instead of relying upon fruit wanting in all these good qualities. The time is at hand when all the peaches for our northern markets will be grown in the North, and every great centre of population will be supplied with its favorite fruit from its immediate surrounding country. This is briefly my experience in peach growing in the North and in the South, on a scale about equal in number of trees cultivated, and which I consider a full, fair and satisfactory test, as shown in the comparative statements made; but as the ground for the first year, in this southern trial at peach growing —or at least twenty acres of it, was planted in strawberries, and was with another orchard of some ten acres occupied in the same way and continued for several years, amply made up for losses that were sustained in the cultivation of peaches in Maryland.

LOCATION AND SOIL.

In treating upon the subject of a location for a peach orchard, as the recommendations are for practical and intelligent farmers, it may be assumed that no one of ordinary intelligence would be likely to select low springy or marshy grounds, as a suitable location for his orchard of peach trees, or for fruit of any kind without thorough ditching and draining. With this hint, the selection ought to be left entirely as an open question, to be decided by the taste and convenience of the planter, as there is little left to choice within the limits of a farm, either of exposure, quality or character of soil as to give any anxiety in a selection. If the proposed orchard should cover the entire farm the question is at once settled. If a field of a few acres only, select high ground and easy of access, and as near to the buildings as may be convenient. As to exposure, North, South, East or West, taking a consecutive number of years, there would be but little difference, if any, as to the protection of the fruit from spring frosts. But I may say, in planting on a small scale, and where a choice of exposures offered, I would unhesitatingly, all other things being equal, select a high, dry northern exposure: for occasionally a season of early blooming occurs, and as the peach is more sensitive to a few days of warm sun on a southern exposure than almost any other fruit, a northern exposure may save the crop, while on the south it may be partially or entirely destroyed; a total destruction, however, is but seldom. I have remarked it but once in forty years, but this difference may occur more frequently on hilly or mountainous regions, where the declivities are great and the exposures have a great difference of temperature. My orchards were on what may be called rolling land, not very hilly, one field about equally divided by a narrow valley, giving the orchard on one side quite a northern exposure, and on the other about the same exposure south. Occasionally I have noticed the crop on the northern exposure the heaviest; but one season, and one only, the crop on the northern exposure was good, while the south was almost an entire failure. My orchards presented almost every exposure, but I have not noted much difference in the effect of frost, except the one I have referred to. In Maryland the land is generally flat, and the question as to exposure does not arise, but even there, there is a choice in location governed mainly by the influence of large bodies of water modifying the temperature and affording in their vicinity protection from late frosts. Such locations are greatly preferred by the peach grower, for although he is south, still he is subject to losses in his fruit crop more so than in Pennsylvania, and the further South we proceed the more precarious and uncertain is the peach crop from the same cause. The peaches raised in Michigan and Wisconsin, for the Chicago market, are principally from orchards cultivated in the vicinity of the lakes, these affording protection to the crop from the severe frosts of spring, and the trees from the severity of winter.

PLANTING.

In preparing the ground for planting, the soil should be deeply broken up, fully to the depth required for setting the trees, when practicable; rocks and stones may be obstacles; follow the plow by a thorough harrowing of the ground; in stiff or clay ground sub-soiling would be of vast advantage. In laying off the rows for planting, which must be done by a heavy plow and a good strong pair of horses, turning the ground up fully to the depth or deeper than the first plowing, so that in cross-checking, the intersection of the furrows, as laid out, will form the holes for planting, only wanting a little filling or leveling with the shovel to prepare them for the tree. With ground prepared in this way, and with four men, and a boy to drop the trees, I have set out 1,000 trees in nine hours. From the time of taking up the trees at the nursery to the time of planting them in the ground prepared for the orchard, there are three very important matters to be observed, and in which there is as much close attention required as at any time in the growth and culture of the tree: First, the protection of the roots from the time of lifting the tree in the nursery; second, the trimming before planting; third, planting properly. By the observance of the following directions at least a year's growth may be saved to the expectant fruit grower—a highly important item in the anticipation of an early return for the labor and capital invested in the new enterprise:

First, the roots of the trees from the time they are lifted at the nursery until planted in the ground, should not be permitted to dry; if transported to a distance, they should be first packed in damp moss, or other material, to keep them damp, and at once shipped with despatch, and on reaching their destination be examined, and if the roots appear dry, they should not be planted until they have been restored by immersion in water from twelve to fourteen hours before planting. If found in good condition in the box, plant them as they are unpacked, and before the roots become dry by exposure. The soaking of the roots in water will restore the small fibres, and the trees, if the weather and soil are favorable, will commence growth at once. It is, I believe, a pretty fair calculation to make, to estimate about one-fourth of the stock taken from the nursery as failing for the want of the observance of more care and attention in the protection of the roots from the taking up to the resetting, and to increase the proportion of losses, there may be much attributed to carelessness in planting. The roots are mostly crowded down into a small, deep hole, twice the depth it should be, and into a cold, poor sub-soil, filling up and settling the earth down by a few shakes of the tree, and thus leaving it to the chances of a dry spring, or a cold wet one, with a dry summer to follow, which is no better for such planting, and there it soon withers and dies.

Instead of such treatment, it should be put in the well pulverized ground at a moderate depth, not deeper than it stood in the nursery, and even not so deep, if the sub-soil in which it is planted is stiff clay; and in all cases, if the tree has been exposed and become dry, soak the roots in water before planting, as above described.

For small peach trees, one year old, and for apples, two and three years old, in planting them, every shovelful of earth should be pressed by the foot firmly to the roots, with *no shaking up and down*, and misplacing and doubling the small roots and fibres, under the old absurd idea, that practical experience never originated or sanctioned. The tree must be established in the first place, firmly in the ground, with the earth impacted about its roots, leaving no room for mould, or other fungi, to conceal themselves for future depredations, and no staking required to keep the tree upright.

In the case of the peach, before planting, the top should be divested of every limb, with a sharp pruning knife, and a portion of the top or main stem, for some four to six inches, leaving the tree in appearance a mere stick above the surface. The latent buds, at the base of the limbs cut off, will break at the opening of the season, and soon show a new and vigorous growth, which, by the fall of the year, will be double the size of the old ones, had they been left, as is generally practiced by amateurs. As a rule, it is advisable, in setting out an orchard or in planting a favorite tree, the owner should superintend the planting or plant himself, unless he has some one to do it on whom he can fully rely, knowing more or as much as he knows himself.

To give an example of faithless employees and bad planting, some years ago I had been employed in setting out some ten to fifteen acres of peach trees, and on the last day of planting, towards evening, I left my men to finish out with some fifty or sixty trees still to be planted. This was on a Saturday afternoon. The trees were put in, and to all appearances, as I observed in a day or two thereafter, they had been planted about as the others had been, but in a short time they gave undoubted evidence that something was wrong with them. There was but here and there one that started in growth. In testing them, as I should have done when I first saw them, and taking hold of one I lifted it out of the ground almost without an effort, and the consequence was that two-thirds of those trees died. This is what the men used to call "covering their tracks," but this case was the last of their "track covering" for me.

In looking into the old authorities, in their recommendations of soils for peach growing, we cannot go amiss in recommending everything, for taking them altogether, we find them running pretty much in the same groove, winding up with the old discriminating degrees of comparison of "good, better, best," the same as our agricultural fairs rank their fruits on exhibition, from the luscious peach to the useful pumpkin, and I think from my experience, I may say that they are all about right, for I have never met with a formation yet upon which I could not succeed in raising peaches; even low, wet, swampy lands can be made to grow them with the proper ditching and draining; but the peach, of all the fruits we grow, adapts itself to more formations and climates than any other species of fruit, from the tropics to the State of Massachusetts, and through all this territory, wherever cultivated, it excels all other fruits grown, for its great beauty, lusciousness and adaptability to the taste, not only of man, but even of the lower animals, birds and insects. From my experience, I can say that it is well adapted to a Gneiss formation, which affords a deep, rich loam, with a small portion of sand, to mica slate, which is composed of quartz and mica, and deposits of talc, to limestone, which is the carbonate of lime, to sandstone and red shale, of slaty structure, composing the red formation passing through the counties of Bucks, Montgomery and Chester, in the State of Pennsylvania, to light sandy soils; also to sandy soils with a red clay subsoil. The most of these, in the course of farm culture, contain more or less rich vegetable mould, and these formations embrace about all the soils of a general geological character constituting our farm lands. These are all adapted to peach culture, but for preference I will name them in the following order: Mica slate, gneiss, red shale, limestone, sandy loam, light sand, sand with red clay subsoil. This last I have tested in Maryland, and there it rates first in quality for peaches or any other fruit. Stiff clay is considered the least desirable, but if well prepared I have found it to produce excellent crops of fruit.

The peach does not require the richest soil. Delaware and Maryland ship thousands of baskets yearly of finely grown peaches from lands below medium quality in fertility. In such soils, and indeed in all soils, the peach requires yearly culture, and with that requisite all soils will produce good peaches in our temperate climate. The peach must make its bearing wood every year, and it requires cultivation to give it strong, vigorous growth.

With fair ground, as to quality, it comes into bearing lightly the third year, if favorable, and in the fourth year I have uniformly, if not cut off by late frosts, had full crops.

My first planting of 1,000 trees produced a full crop the fourth year, and attracted a great deal of interest from a doubting community for miles around, disarming all the threadbare arguments that peaches could not be raised in Chester county. There was scarcely a year in which the crop entirely failed, and a partial crop often brings more than a full one. In such years peaches are scarce, and the market prices are correspondingly higher. I have had peaches to retail in the Philadelphia market as high as seventy-five cents per dozen, direct from my orchards, and they have often since brought higher prices from Chester county orchards. Those who have read Edwin Morris' admirable little book, entitled "Ten Acres Enough," will recollect that he tells us of his ten old peach trees in his garden, which, after supplying the family with fruit for the season, realized sixty to seventy dollars for the surplus fruit sent to market.

CULTIVATION.

The peach of all the fruits has for the last fifty years made better return for good and careful cultivation and labor expended, than all the other fruits for market purposes within reach of our northern cities. It will pay better than any crop on the farm and from my experience nothing I believe will pay the farmer better for the money and labor expended than its cultivation. The idea is prevalent at the North that in the healthy districts in Maryland and the South the tree springs up and without culture or care grows up and flourishes in health and productiveness for almost an indefinite period, but this is a mistake, as the apple and other fruits which we see there running into old age have had their culture in the rotation of field crops and if standing in gardens they have had their annual culture incidentally with the cultivation of the flowering plants and vegetables. Under these circumstances we see these old relics of a past century from three up to seven feet in circumference of body, and two to two and a half feet around in limbs, still responding faithfully in good crops of fruit almost yearly for the little care bestowed upon them. Many of them through a long life of sacred associations are still the object of family endearment. Why should not care and culture prolong the life of the tree as it does that of our permanent plants and the common products of the earth? Fruitfulness and longevity require culture and without it both vegetable and animal life would result in failure. And here we read the history of our failure through our own prejudices and lack of energy years ago to grow this delicious fruit in Pennsylvania during its almost entire culture beyond the limits of our State and to be taken up by the early pioneers of the enterprise—the citizens of Delaware and Maryland, as a branch of common industry and one which has added its millions of dollars to their agricultural interests in raising them to competence and affluence in a fifty years undisturbed monopoly of our markets. I do not speak of this in any feeling of complaint, for they deserve it all for their energy and their labor. Their foresight stands as a monument to their perseverance and industry. As we are now, with our discoveries, placed on an equal footing, so far as to say that we, too, can raise peaches at home, and compete with them in our own markets, we may now congratulate ourselves in the hope that the time is coming when we may, in some measure, return the many obligations to our friends in Delaware at least by catering to their tastes in the markets of Wilmington, the growing metropolis of their State.

The planting of peach trees will not interfere, to

any appreciable amount, with the crop of corn, by turning down, as usual, a stiff sod, and in planting the peach trees at 16x18 feet in the rows we will have one hundred and fifty to the acre. Using that many hills of corn, the corn being planted 3x4 at, say eighty bushels to the acre, the one hundred and fifty hills occupied by the trees would reduce the product of the acre only about three and one-half bushels. The second year we put in corn, potatoes and other crops, requiring culture, also manuring in the hill to make the corn crop, and this second year's crop may not exceed over two-thirds that of the first year; the third year to be again planted with corn, or such crops as require cultivation, and after the third year all cropping to be suspended, but the field or orchard thereafter to be cultivated by plowing and harrowing it at least once a year, and oftener in years of overbearing, as hereinafter pointed out.

MANURES.

As the analysis of the peach, apple and pear shows them so nearly allied in proportional quantities of the most important elements of which they are composed, on the settled principle that these constituent parts indicate the food upon which they exist, it is evident that in catering to their appetites, we may feed them all from a compost formed of the same fertilizing elements of which they are mainly composed. Every suitable soil of medium fertility contains a sufficient quantity of the requisite elements for a healthy and vigorous growth of the peach; therefore, but little, if any, of the fertilizing elements will be required at planting, or in its growth up to bearing, unless as a precaution against infection from that fell specific disease, the "yellows," to which it is subject in Pennsylvania, and in the most of our neighboring States. The following is a chemical analysis of the peach, apple and pear, the leading fruits adapted to our soil and climate:

Peach—Potash, 12; lime, 23; phosphate of lime, 21.

Apple—Potash, 16; lime, 19; phosphate of lime, 17.

Pear—Potash, 22; lime, 13; phosphate of lime, 27.

It will be observed that there is but little difference in the chemical composition of these important elements, except that of lime, which, in the peach, is largely developed. All these ingredients are familiar to every tiller of the soil as manures, and are applied almost yearly to crops. With this analysis before us, we have no need of inquiry of our neighbor as to the kind of manure best adapted to the orchard. We see that these three fruits are composed largely of potash, lime and phosphate of lime, and when the soil becomes exhausted of either, or all, and the ground begins to present the appearance of poverty, as indicated in the crop, these elements must be resupplied to restore the trees, or rather to continue their growth and vigor.

In medium soils an application of *caustic* or *quick lime*, direct from the kiln, at the rate of fifty bushels to the acre, spread on the plowed ground, and well harrowed in, as for corn, is about all the manuring or treatment that the ground requires for the peach tree at planting, and for the first season of its growth, with the usual attention in cultivating the corn, potatoes or other cultivated crops which may occupy the ground. As caustic lime—always cheap and accessible—is to act a leading part in the new programme, as a remedial agent for the protection of the health of the peach tree from its specific disease, in connection with other alkalies, it may be as well for us to look now somewhat into its chemical and mechanical action in the multiple economy of vegetable life. Lime may be employed to prevent the decay of wood and other organic substances, or it may be employed for their decomposition. We have the example of the first in ships and wooden structures used in transportation of burned lime, and in carts and wagons conveying it from the kiln to the fields. In these cases the lime is in excess of the organic matter, and therefore the moisture in the wood is absorbed by the lime, while the fibre is preserved in this way from decomposition; but if these conditions are reversed, and the water and organic matter are in excess of the newly burned lime, the wood will decay. Lime is employed on our soils to reduce or decompose vegetable elements, to correct its acidity, or for the solution of silica, or the decomposition of iron salts in the soil.

Lime has a powerful attraction for carbonic acid, and as vegetable matter is composed largely of carbon, it is readily seen why decomposition takes place. Quick or caustic lime, in fact, soon becomes the carbonate of lime by exposure to the action of vegetable matter, and thus loses its caustic properties. As an alkali, lime neutralizes acidity in the soil, and sweetens it for the growth of our crops. A good soil must not possess any acid properties.

The remains of plants, and even stable manure are of an acid nature, but the soil usually contains, in its mineral constituents, so many bases—lime, potash, soda and magnesia—that these suffice to neutralize the acidity. But when this natural supply is insufficient we must add to it, and lime is the cheapest base at the hands of the farmer. Lime has the property of setting at liberty the alkalies in the soil, thus favoring the formation of the soluble silicates, so important to the growth of grass and grain. The application of lime to land and the burning of clay act on the same principle in decomposing the clay silicates and liberating their alkalies, thus favoring solubility and affording nutriment to vegetable life. Lime in its caustic state is destructive to *moss, lichen, fungi* and all vegetable and animal matter.

In the month of October the fields of Yorkshire, and Oxfordshire, England, look as if they were covered with snow. They are plowed down, and whole square miles are seen whitened over with *quick lime*, which during the moist winter months exercises its beneficial influence upon the stiff clay soil of those countries.

Fruitfulness in cold clay soils may be promoted and made equal to the best for apples, peaches and other fruits with a moderate dressing of *quick lime*, about the quantity such lands should receive for corn. Lime will generally promote profuse flowering and fruiting of trees and plants, the lime salts producing evaporation and concentration of the sap. On the black vegetable lands of southern Maryland, with caustic oyster shell lime of forty bushels to the acre, fifty bushels of corn can be produced to the acre without using a shovel full of other manure. The quick lime neutralizes the acid in the sour vegetable soil sweetening it and changing it into rich soluble food for the crop. The cultivated plants which consume very much lime in their development will naturally lead much sooner to an exhaustion of the lime in the soil, than those plants which use lime only moderately.

These brief references to the chemical and mechanical operations of lime on the vegetable and mineral substances in the soil, will give us some idea of its importance in preparing the soil with indispensible food to the healthy growth of plants and trees.

The questions as to the time, condition and quantity in which this great corrective alkaline agent should be applied to the soil to obtain the most desirable results are of vast importance to the interests of the country. Many an agricultural crop has been lost and many an orchard has withered and died for the want of a better knowledge of that class of alkaline manures which make up so largely the elements of vegetable growth. It will be observed that the analysis has given us but three of the ingredients, among the many, which go to make up the entire composition of the peach and the other fruits named, viz: potash, lime and phosphate of lime, these being the important ones, and the only ones indeed required to enable us to point out the requisite manures; the others being supplied in small quantities already in the soil or obtained from the atmosphere.

In the analysis of the peach, apple and pear referred to, potash ranks as the second ingredient of importance, entering largely as a component part of these three leading fruits. We will here briefly present it as another of the alkaline agents with quick lime active in the destruction of the relentless enemy to the peach tree. In speaking of potash we associate it at once with ashes as they are well known to contain largely of this element, and they are all at the command of the farmer that furnish it.

Practice has shown that Potash exerts a highly favorable influence on the growth of plants. The Chemist informs us that potash belongs to the caustic alkaline bodies and in this form resembles ammonia, and this similarity is carried out in its strong action in forcing vegetable growth. The virgin soil furnishes us with potash and it will continue to do so, for all kinds of earth and stone contain stores of it in an insoluble state, and a certain portion is made soluble from year to year by the weather and our plants have the benefit of this. Spreading the fields over with *quick lime* causes an increased quantity of potash, since lime possesses the power of decomposing rocks and stones containing it (Stockhart Ag. Chem.) But if the soil is employed from year to year in the growth of exhaustive crops, the salts of potash must to some extent be given back in some form to prevent the land from becoming sterile for the want of this important element of which it has been robbed. An example we have in the exhausted soils of Virginia by the successive crops of tobacco grown by the early settlers of the country who looked upon the virgin soil of their farms as inexhaustible—and as also the farmers in the rich Genesee Valley of New York, within my recollection, entertained the same views. In advertising their farms for sale, one of the advantages claimed was that the barn and stables were located on a stream of water sufficient to carry off the manure without the trouble and expense of carting. Although this may be so with a continued succession of exhaustive crops, (all crops are exhaustive if all is taken off and nothing returned,) for the potash and other manurial ingredients will go faster than the weather can annually supply them. But this is not the case with our orchards, for it is well known that a peach orchard improves the soil and it is the same with the apple and pear orchards as may be seen in the soil for years after they have died out or been removed. I believe that an analysis of the soils of any of our orchards would show as much if not more lime and potash than they could have done at the planting; however old they may be if not exhausted by overcropping; for the continual stirring of the soil as in the peach orchard and the turning in yearly with the plow all vegetable growth, that may be made through the growing season, and the fallen foliage of the trees in the fall; together with the exposure of the soil to the decomposing actions of rains and frost and other atmospheric influences, make soluble that which was before insoluble for the support of plants. From rock and stone and pebble and grains of sand, down even below a microscopic atom is developed this important agent, potash, which plays its incomprehensible role in the support of vegetable and animal life. All these elements are at work in their proper seasons, furnishing lime, potash and other alkalies to the soil, the same as we observe in Virginia for the past century, furnishing slowly but surely a returning supply of plant food to be husbanded, it is to be hoped, more carefully for the present and succeeding generations.

We may assume that the peach, apple and pear contained in their first introduction into the country the same quantities and relative proportion of ingredients in their composition that they now do, and that no complaint was then made in the North that the soil had become exhausted of its potash and lime; nor is there any complaint now in the South where the orchards thrive and produce from fifty to sixty years. The shortened life and failure in the North arose from another cause, which was noticed and first recorded by Judge Peters, the President of the "Philadelphia Agricultural Society," who, on the 11th of February, 1806, in a communication to the Society, wrote: "About fifty years ago, on the farm on which I now reside, my father had a large peach orchard which yielded abundantly until a general catastrophe befel it. Plentiful crops had been for many years produced with but little attention, when the trees all at once began to decline and finally perished. For forty years past I have observed the peach trees in my neighborhood to be short lived." This sudden transition from a long life to a short one was not from the exhaustion of the soil. It was from disease, and in the peach tree the great and overshadowing disease caused by a "parasitic fungi," and perhaps from slighter injuries from insect life. *These pests being destroyed, the orchard will be restored to its primitive health, thrift, productiveness and a more prolonged life.*

The remedy is at hand in the very elements which afford food for the tree, and of which it is mainly composed—lime, potash and other alkalies, and while giving life and strength to the tree they are striking down and removing the cause of disease, when properly applied.

In recommending a suitable manure for the peach, and following out the indications shown by the analysis, and my own experience, I may say that "*caustic or quick lime is now for the first time publicly announced as an indispensable specific remedial agent, with the other alkalies named, against the yellows in the peach tree.*"

In seasons of *overbearing* the orchard should be cultivated up to about the *middle of July* with the plow or cultivator and harrow, the same as with the young trees before their bearing and while cultivated in corn; and if apparently needing manure a light shovelful of wood ashes applied to the tree at its base—first removing the earth from around it with a heavy hoe—and this course of treatment will keep the trees in a thrifty, growing condition, forming wood for the next year's crop, and sustaining them through their exhaustive efforts under an over cropping. But this unnatural draft upon the strength of the tree may be avoided, under a judicious thinning out of the young fruit to a moderate crop. This is done to a limited extent occasionally, but I have never yet known it to be extended to large orchards. There can be no doubt of the advantage and profit of such a practice, as a case in point from a successful gardener shows: "My ten fruit trees were loaded with fruit. When as large as hickory nuts, I began the operation of removing all the smallest, and of thinning out unsparingly wherever they were crowded. After going over five trees in this way, in deference to gentle remonstrances from his 'better half,' he suspended his 'ravages,' leaving five untouched.

In summing up he states that the peaches on the five denuded trees grew prodigiously large. These were gathered and sent to the Philadelphia market and brought forty-one dollars clear of all expenses, while the fruit from the other five trees, sent to market, netted only twenty-six dollars, making a difference of fifteen dollars in favor of thinning. The ten trees produced sixty-seven dollars, but if all had been thinned the product would have been eighty-two dollars.

This difference, extended to an orchard of 10,000 to 20,000 trees, would make a handsome annual profit. This is a striking illustration, though it might not be carried out on a large scale, at so high a rate, still it is a hard fact in favor of expending a little labor to a large profit. This is an impressive example for our fruit growers and gardeners, but more particularly to those on a limited scale, who can in some measure make up in quality what they lack in quantity. I expect however that the matter is pretty well adjusted as it is giving the advantage to the small though careful producer in his quality. Where there is a will there is a way and with the enthusiast it is a well beaten path to the object of his ambition.

In applying manures to trees and plants, when required, if the compost heap, or the means to procure the requisite elements recommended, fall short of a supply for the entire surface of the garden or orchard, the object may be attained by adopting the

"Chinese method" of manuring the roots rather than the soil, by applying the fertilizing liquid or solid to the base of the tree by first removing the earth from around it, giving it, in the case of the peach, a shovelful of wood ashes occasionally, or soap-suds, lime, poudrette, or a little composted guano, or other alkali, graduating the quantity to the strength of the application and size of the tree. This will give better immediate results than ten times the quantity scattered broadcast on the surface, as around the base of the tree the application is at once direct to the proper place, and will soon show the effect on the orchard. My views on this point are contained in an article submitted at a meeting of the Fruit Grower's Society of Pennsylvania, held at Reading, January 15, 1873, and published in the proceedings of the society, in volume 9, of the Pennsylvania State Agricultural Society, inquiring as to the "Best Method of Manuring Fruit Trees, Their Appropriate Manures, &c." from which the following is extracted:

"Perhaps it is enough to apply the remedy direct to the roots of the trees around their trunk, instead of treating all the soil of the orchard; experiments, as shown, seem to have established this fact. With my experiments with ashes, charcoal, poudrette, also with lime, the application around the tree, first removing the earth from the surface, I have found quite sufficient; the potash or other alkalies being absorbed and carried into the circu lation, and in the course of a few months a new supply of fine surface roots from the tree encircling the whole stock, spreading in every direction in the alkaline compost, and taking up the nutritious elements they contain, increasing the thrift and fruitfulness of the tree. Here we have the evidence that this portion of the tree, at least, absorbs nutriment as well as the roots and leaves, and that every portion of the tree performs the same office."

This practice is directly in the teeth of the theory of Professor Lindley, (England's great vegetable physiologist), in his facetious ridicule in the closing page of his work on "Horticulture," in which he says:

"I have seen a gardener, who ought to have known much better, seduously administering liquid manure, by pouring it into the soil at the base of the stem, which is much the same thing as if an attempt were made to feed a man through the soles of his feet."

There is not, I would suppose, an intelligent farmer in Chester county but who could convince the old philosopher of the error implied in his ridicule of the wise gardener, nor is there a doctor within the same limits but would confirm it practically, by the insertion of a little solution of morphia in the professor's back for lumbago. I may here add that the Chinese system of manuring by a direct application, as the manure of the professor's gardener, is the most plausible argument that can be used for the gross system of culture, which has its distinguished advocates; but I find none among extensive peach growers who break the soil yearly.

It has always been remarked that quality, and not quantity, is what is wanted. My observation has been that beauty outranks quantity, in the fruit market, at least. To present that requisite in more than its natural attraction, I would recommend an occasional manuring of the ground around the tree with ammoniacal manures, such as guano, poudrette, and with charcoal, which is a heavy absorbent of ammonia. These elements, through their ammonia, will impart to the peach an intensity to that peculiar rich, deep mellow red color, known to no other fruit, giving it its great beauty over all others; and in addition to this, these ammoniacal elements are, in their effects, highly enriching to the soil, as we are all aware, and as strong *alkalies* act as remedial agents against the "yellows." The expense of fertilizers for the culture of the peach is much less than for any other crop on the farm. My practice was to a considerable extent to plant apple orchards in the grounds occupied in peach trees. The trees are cultivated together, and the fertilizers of the one are adapted to the other, and in some six or eight years the apples will begin to bear, and there will be but little interference, the apple trees being planted in rows 22x36, the peach trees 16x18. My large orchards were mostly planted 18x18 feet. I have tried them at from 12x12 up to 18x20, but finally settled down to 18x18, which I found to be about the proper distance; intersecting the orchard with roads at convenient distances for gathering the fruit, small orchards not requiring such an arrangement, the head lands being wide enough for wagons to pass and repass in removing fruit.

INTRODUCTORY TO THE FOLLOWING CHAPTER ON THE INDICATIONS OF THE YELLOWS:

The subject of the "yellows" in the peach tree has come under the notice of the Agricultural Department at Washington, and recognized as a question of great importance to our agricultural interests. The microscopist of the Department, Prof. Thomas Taylor, in his investigations into the cause of this wide spread and most destructive disease, has thrown around the whole subject many new and interesting features that seem to have harmonized our Pomologists, and led to the adoption of Prof. Taylor's conclusions, that *Fungi* is the cause of this fatal disease. These microscopic reports of the investigations of Prof. Taylor, accompanied by illustrations, will be found at length in the Agricultural Reports of the Department for the years 1871 and '72. We understand that further examinations are being made by the Department, which, no doubt, will go to confirm the conclusions to which the former investigations led. This, it is hoped, will settle the great question which has baffled the untiring efforts of the country for almost the last century to discover a *cause*.

We have now only to apply a remedy in a

proper way to restore our diseased peach districts and sections of the country to a healthy condition as peach growing regions, and I think that this may be found in my practice of treatment in peach growing for the last thirty years, and as recommended here in these pages with the vigilant precautions I have pointed out.

INDICATION OF YELLOWS.

In the yellows the bearing tree in its incipient stage of disease shows a *premature ripening* of the fruit, sometimes only in a single branch, or even a fruit spur, and on other trees the fruit on a large limb may present the same early maturity, while in both trees the balance of the fruit retains its natural green, thrifty condition, and to all appearances perfectly healthy, but as the disease progresses the fruit continues to be affected gradually in the same way up to the ripening of the healthy crop. I have known many fruit growers to be deceived with these appearances, supposing that in this early maturity they had a new variety of great value, which could be increased by inoculation; and for a time the supposed new fruit was quietly spoken of in a very confidential way. But alas! the next year's appearance of both fruit and tree fully dispelled the delusion, and instead of a new early variety, the disappointment ended in a crop of small astringent, worthless fruit and a tree in the advanced stage of the disease. The most of our authors inform us that the fruit indicating the disease is smaller than the healthy fruit. My experience uniformally has been that in the first stages of the disease, where but a few peaches on a tree ripen prematurely, they are much larger than mature fruit of the general crop of the same variety. I well recollect, and will here cite one or two cases of trees slightly affected, which produced fruit of immense size:

At the first exhibition of the Chester County Horticultural Society, held at West Chester, Pa., early in September, 1848, Mr. B. Graves exhibited a few specimens of the Red Cheek Malacaton, which for size and beauty could not have been excelled, many of them measuring thirteen inches in circumference, but all exhibited here and there on the surface the fatal symptoms of disease, manifested by deep reddish, purple splotches and hectic spots, in beautiful contrast with that rich tint peculiar only to this delicate fruit. This, of course, was the first and the last contribution from that noble tree, and it fell prematurely under this fatal disease that has seldom spared its victim.

There was exhibited at the same time a beautiful collection of the same variety from an orchard near Chester Springs, which also showed slight indications of the same disease. These took a premium, and were sent directly to the Horticultural Fair then open in Philadelphia, and there also received the premium for their great size and beauty, and as I was informed, were considered a *valuable seedling* and *not* the Malacaton as labelled. Hundreds of bushels of these prematurely ripened peaches from badly diseased trees are sold in the early markets, bringing prices much greater perhaps than the healthy crop, on account of their early ripening, and hence it is that diseased trees are left standing in yards and gardens and even in the orchards of some peach districts, diffusing their poisonous contagion throughout an entire district, blasting their own and their neighbor's healthy trees, in order that they may at so great sacrifice gather from their dying plants the last deserted and tasteless peach. The disease in its earliest stages in young trees, which, by the way, sometimes comes from the nursery in the stock we purchase, is more difficult to detect than at a later period.

It requires a practical eye and a knowledge of the habits of the tree to detect it, and its peculiar features, as there are several active agents at work which may cause the yellow appearance, and the casual observer might be mistaken; and through this very common mistake we have so many different and infallible recipes for the cure of the yellows. The next indication, and the only one by which the majority of peach growers first detect the disease, is as indicative and as marked in its symptoms of approaching death as the "black vomit" in the human system. This next indication to which we now refer, is seen in the small wiry shoots springing from the body and large branches, or from the roots at the base of the tree, producing in every instance small yellow lanceolate (lance-like) leaves, and the whole tree assuming a sickly appearance in leaves and branches, and producing small highly colored fruit with the peculiar spots and blotches as before described, only more numerous with flesh deep red and stringy, and fruit worthless for any purpose of family use or for marketing. I am so entirely familiar with the appearance of the diseased peach tree in all its stages, that I can readily tell the condition of an orchard by examining a few general samples of its fruit at maturity, either premature or healthy. In a special disease the discovery of the cause may be the means of leading to the discovery of a cure, but if the special remedy be known, the doctor can get along with the patient without troubling himself so much with the cause of disease. It is pretty generally believed that the cause here arises from a Parasitic Fungi in the bark and roots of the tree, but it is not for us just here to discuss that question, nor is it at all necessary, as we know our remedy and the course of treatment to be applied, which has proven entirely satisfactory in raising fruit on a large scale for twelve or fifteen years consecutively in the same orchards in Chester and Delaware counties, surrounded at the same time by thousands of trees, dead and dying from the disease for the want of the application of proper measures, and quite as much, perhaps, from the want of care and proper treatment. My large and successful orchards were intersected by public roads much traveled, and were the cause of great attraction, exciting an interest that led to the planting of thousands of trees, but as our apple orchards are now cultivated and cared for, these new plantings of the peach were generally left to take the rotation of farm crops, of corn, oats, wheat and clover, and they soon yielded and finally fell victims to the borer and the yellows.

The disease is communicated by contact of roots, inoculation or trimming. A knife used on a diseased tree will communicate the disease if used on a healthy one. If the disease arises from Parasitic Fungi, it is most likely communicated by what is called sporadic contagion. A great deal of the cause of its rapid spread, no doubt, may be attributed to the practice so prevalent with peach growers in the annual trimming of their orchards. It has no doubt been ruinous to those growers who have not been able to recognize the disease in its early stages. Only the trimming of a few diseased trees in an orchard may be the means of spreading the disease over the entire orchard in the course of two or three years, and this would more likely be the case if the trimming should be done in the spring or summer at the full circulation and flow of the sap. Really the tree wants but little trimming after the head is formed. This is to be regulated according to taste and convenience. My practice has been to head my trees leaving the body five to six feet in length, so as to cultivate with freedom and ease with small horses or mules, well up to the tree, thus saving much labor and affording a free circulation of air and a full view through an orchard of considerable size. Low heading makes close and neat cultivation rather difficult and more expensive, and what is worse than all liable to be neglected. The peach grower looking to success which is found alone in the health of his trees must be a bold operator. On the first symptoms of disease if only in a twig or a fruit spur, it must be eradicated, root body and branch, and as the barren fig tree cast into the fire, renewing its place by first applying to the soil in which it grew the necessary curative manures in sufficient quantity for a healthy reception for a new tree at the proper season for planting.

Shall we longer as advised by the old school of vegetable Philosophers still wait the old cycle of time—20 years—to renew a removed apple or peach tree, or replant a new orchard on the ground following the removal of the old? I am prepared to answer no; with the light before us we will treat our orchards as we treat our crops; rotate at a time and in a way to suit our own convenience, and not to suit the tastes and convenience of fungoid toadstools and infusoria, our enemies in peach growing and so insignificant too, that we have to use 500 or 1000 diameter microscopic power to bring them within the range of our vision.

"Nature abhors a vacuum," so said the old Philosophers; their successors said nature did no such thing and proved it. We can point to farmers as a class residing within one hundred miles of the city of Philadelphia, who let their corn land rest every alternate year, while the farmers in Pennsylvania found out long ago that they could not afford their lands any such indulgence; each field must produce a crop annually and respond liberally to good treatment. This is the course to be pursued in peach growing and this is what we intend to do. We have found out long ago through dearly bought experience that the system of "masterly inactivity" never did nor never will pay in farming at least. Whether the peach is a long lived or a short lived tree, or a large tree or a small tree we shall not stop here to enquire, but we intend to make it produce as long at least as our faithful horse labors on the farm, or our generous dairy cow affords us milk and what more could we ask of the peach? With care and exemption from disease we may double the period of its production, for such is its longevity in the healthy districts not one hundred miles south of Philadelphia, that we can reasonably look for a more extended limit. Why then should not the peach be permitted a place on the farm, and raised to the dignity of a new staple for Pennsylvania, and *at once* for the counties contiguous to our great markets supplying the annual want which is now supplied from adjoining States? From the quick return of the crop under careful culture of four short years, the six counties of Delaware, Chester, Montgomery, Bucks, Berks and Lancaster, may reap a rich harvest from the product of the peach orchard, increasing yearly, to meet the increasing consumption and in a little while yielding more in profits than any other branch of farm industry, not excepting Lancaster's great staple—tobacco.

PEACH BORER, &C.

The Peach worm or borer is a four winged insect, wasp like in shape, and of a steel blue color. It deposits its eggs from early in the summer until fall, near the ground around the base of the tree. The young larva or worm enters the bark at the root of the tree and for the whole year subsisting on and ringing the tree if not attended to, and in the spring having finished its ravages encases itself in a gum and saw dust like envelope or cocoon, under the bark or just beneath the earth, around the door of its premises, soon to change from pupa to insect life. It rarely happens that healthy trees are entirely destroyed by it unless greatly neglected. As it confines its depredations to the bark not entering the wood it is easily captured and destroyed on examination in the fall if carefully done, and the larva removed by a sharp pointed knife; and about an *ounce* of *hard soap* firmly rubbed around the base of the tree an inch or so beneath the surface and if about the same quantity be applied to the place injured by the worm or in the incision made by the knife it would be of great benefit in healing over the wound and giving growth and vigor to the tree.

The potash in this case has its direct application

to the sap circulation and is the very kind of food the little wiry surface roots are looking after in the soil to carry to the limbs, leaves and fruit. Here again is an application of the "Chinese system" of manuring the tree instead of the soil. These two ounces of soap (potash) will do more good to the tree than a half a bushel of ashes sown on the bare surface of the ground broadcast, and it will be as effective in keeping off the borer through the season.

The cheapest and most efficient and expeditious way to keep an orchard clear of the peach worm or borer, is the plan above recommended of removing it with a knife and applying an ounce or two of cheap hard soap. The application of the soap, while it repels the insect and borer is a powerful stimulant to the tree, and acts quickly and efficiently. Other enemies that commit their depredations on the limbs, branches and leaves of the tree, though slight compared to the yellows, such as curled leaf, mildew, &c., &c., destructive to small limbs, call for their remedies also. Strong soap suds, or a solution of potash and urine will destroy mildew, fungi, aphides, bark insects, &c. Whatever is effective to the root is also beneficial to the branches. I have always found whitewash sufficient, and in looking at the many recommendations by practical Pomologists I find they all make *lime* the leading ingredient, and it seems that lime and potash are indeed about all that is required to produce the required effect, which is to destroy the parasitic agents, insects and fungi on the limbs, body and leaves of the tree. A good wash for the limbs and body of the tree is a half a peck of unslacked lime, one quart of soft soap, and pour on this warm water until it comes to the consistence of whitewash, and apply with a brush. If the whitewash is objectionable it can be changed to any color desired. Others have recommended about the same composition; adding, however, sulphur, soot and various compounds, but the vital destructive agents in all such washes are the lime and potash.

PRUNING.

I have already elsewhere remarked that the peach really requires very little of what is generally understood as pruning or trimming after the head of the tree is properly formed, except to keep all sprouts or shoots cut or rubbed off as they appear springing from the roots at the collar of the tree or from the main body. The first pruning or trimming is to the young tree, after it arrives from the nursery and before planting, which has been fully described. The system of shortening the branches and limbs as practised among amateurs, gardeners and small growers, though employed to but a limited extent, if judiciously applied, is productive of very satisfactory results. It is, indeed, but a counterpart to plowing, which is a shortening in of the roots; both performing important parts in perpetuating thrift, productiveness and life of the tree, and more particularly in diseased districts, and under the present system of peach growing which has undergone but little change of importance for the past fifty years at least, the tree for a little time producing, though holding out but a false hope, then lingering and dying under its fatal disease the yellows. In such cases this double cutting in by the plow at the roots and the knife at the limbs, destroying or palliating for a time to a considerable extent the incipient stage of the disease in the tree, whether it arises from the agency of an insect or from the ravages of a parasitic fungi; in either case it affects the body and branches as well as the roots of the tree. While the plow cuts and turns up the entire network of surface roots, and destroys as well the active agent of disease, the knife performs a like office by cutting in the limbs and branches, destroying to a large extent the active agent there, thus divesting the tree to the extent of the loss of its diseased roots and branches of the fell enemy, leaving the tree in its full flow of sap to throw out its thousands of new surface roots as feeders to work in the more healthy soil which has just been turned down by the plow. The shortened limbs in the new growth now in active sympathy with the roots, respond in a more healthy current of sap—the life-blood of the tree—in a vigorous growth of wood and root for another year of productiveness.

This system of culture of the peach tree, plowing and cutting in the branches, with the addition of a bold operation in eradicating the diseased trees, if any, as they appear, attended by its reversing effects of health and returning vigor, is one among the strong evidences that this infection is caused by fungi. A pruning of the roots and a judicious cutting of the branches and limbs in the way I have pointed out, and for the reason assigned, and even in the application of remedial agents, prevention of the disease would be more benefit to the orchard than any blind empirical course of the highest culture that could be adopted.

The large peach-growers, most of whom are on the healthy side of the peach-dividing line between the North and South, are exempt from the evils referred to, and they have not adopted this course of shortening in to any extent, leaving the orchard after the proper heading, pretty much to its natural growth, attending rather to the necessary thinning out of all intruding sprouts, and removing dead and dying branches, leaving the tree as described by one of our distinguished Pomologists, "when in fruit with bending slender branches in graceful curves, so as to open the spreading heads and let in the sun and air to color up the fruit, all through the middle of the tree as well as the outside." "This is the plan," he further observes, "which is found to work much better than heading the tree in." As this mode, it seems, has become almost a universal system and has worked well, and having its convenience, it will be continued there with large peach growers, while the heading-in system will be practised North among amateurs, gardeners and small producers. It is evident that a tree judiciously cut in, and the fruit thinned in years of overbearing, will produce fruit under good cultivation of increased size and improved in quality, which will command a much higher price in the market than the general crop under ordinary care.

*These are all questions that enter into the consideration of labor, expense and time consumed, and are for each one to decide for himself. The active, energetic, vigilant and farsighted man in the peach, as well as in every other enterprise, will avail himself of all the advantages to be derived to the extent of his ability, and will adopt such a system as will prove to the greatest advantage between expense and profit.

---

* Well directed pruning is one of the most useful, and if ill directed, it is among the most mischevious operations that can take place in application to a tree.

THE VALUE OF PEACH GROWING.

There is no crop that can be raised with less labor and expense, and a quicker return, than that of the peach, and none that will give a greater return for the capital and labor employed. The peach farms in Upper Delaware and Maryland, have returned to their owners the most fabulous amounts for their investments, far exceeding in profit any other staple crop that has been raised in the Middle States, and on a scale never before heard of in this or any other country. Some of the orchards containing from 1,000 to 1,300 acres have netted their owners from $20,000 to $30,000 annually. A peach orchard in New Castle county, Delaware, of 400 acres, netted the owner in one crop, $38,000. One in Kent county, Maryland, of some 600 acres, produced a crop paying $31,000, and the same orchard in 1879, yielded $42,000. In 1873, the Delaware Peach Growers' Association, reported that there were sent from the Delaware peninsula to the northern markets of Philadelphia, and New York, 1,288,500 baskets of peaches, or 2,577 car loads by the railroad. Adding the quantity shipped by steamers and sailing vessels, and the amount canned, the actual quantity amounted, in the aggregate, to 2,000,000 of baskets. In 1872, the whole district, comprising the Eastern Shore of Maryland, marketed, 3,500,000 baskets. The late Col. Wilkins, on Chester river, Kent county, Maryland, had 1,350 acres in with peach trees, numbering 137,000, producing in bearing years from $30,000 to $40,000 annually. In the State of Michigan peach growing is carried on to a considerable extent, along the shores of the lake, some sixty miles from Chicago, and furnishes the fruit to the city and surrounding towns. It is reported that Mr. A. T. Dykeman, President of the Horticultural Society of the State, in 1873, sold peaches to the amount of $10,000 from sixty-five acres, and in 1872 a grower from six acres received $1,700.

Peaches are grown to a fine profit in Wisconsin, for Chicago. All these western districts, including Ohio, Indiana and other States, complain of the ravages of the yellows, and the Legislature of Wisconsin has even passed an act to prevent the spread of the disease, and I am informed that the law works well. Thousands of dollars have been invested by individual enterprise in planting and cultivating the pear, and although we hear, in every direction, of its failure in dwarf trees, still the markets seem to be pretty well supplied through the fruit season, yet at low prices, and particularly when it comes in competition with the peach, which, during the past season, was very marked. I noticed in the market at West Chester, and also in Philadelphia, baskets of first class Bartlett pears, in fine condition, by the side of Delaware peaches; the pears were going off slowly at fifty cents per basket, while the peaches were readily bringing seventy-five cents. As a market fruit for production and profit the pear pales before the peach—the expense and extra culture required in producing good pears is never returned in the product to half the profits of the peach—and again the long time required before it is brought into a bearing condition, is one of the great drawbacks to pear culture.

> He who plants pears,
> Plants for his heirs.

But notwithstanding all these disadvantages to be met with by the enthusiast in pear culture, I have, at different times, set out some 3,000 trees, dwarf and standard, for orchard culture, but they have not been satisfactory. The pear is sold by the single specimen, while the peach is sold by the crate or basket. Many of the large estates in Lower Maryland and Delaware, which were originally purchased for a few dollars per acre, are now fortunes to their owners. On my last visit to the Raybold orchards, at Delaware city, I was informed by the Colonel, that he had then some 700 acres in peach trees, and some 500 acres were then in bearing. Crosby Morton, on the Chester river, at Round Top, had some 1,000 acres in trees, and he informed me that in a settlement between him and his partner of the receipts of the season's crop they divided near $50,000 between them. These net profits from these large orchards seem immense, but smaller growers greatly exceed in the rate of profits, owing to the greater and more economical facility of handling, and the ability of doing it, as everything can be managed with system and economy, and without the loss that occurs from dependence upon others. The encouraging feature of the peach business is in its almost unlimited extent and ever increasing demand, and necessarily so from the unlimited wants of our improving towns and country. Peaches are marketed by the millions of baskets, where apples and other fruits are counted only by the thousands. The large peach grower must be a landholder; and, like the merchant, he has his large aggregate profits, and correspondingly large expenses and losses in the management of business, while the small peach grower, in most cases, in counties contiguous to large cities, would manage the orchard and its products under his own eye from the field to the market, making the best of everything and doubling his profits. The great peach growers of Delaware and Maryland are looked upon as the Wanamakers of the orchards, though with goods not "marked," while the small producer has his brands for superior quality on the cheek of his ripe, luscious fruit, to be disposed of in a comparatively retail market. The one sells in the field, by the orchard or the crop, the other by the basket and the peck, obtaining larger prices and better profits.

If this should meet the eye of any one who has become tired or worn out with farming, and is desirous of disposing of his farm, I would advise him to plant from ten to fifteen acres in peach trees, and at the same time a suitable portion with apple trees among the peaches at proper distances apart. Such an improvement in two or three years, or just at bearing, will secure a purchaser at a greatly enhanced price, paying more than one thousand per cent. on the cost of the orchard. In this I have had a great deal of experience, as I have never failed in putting in a good orchard as the first improvement on the many farms I have purchased, if I found they wanted it. I have found it as a general rule that nothing is more attractive to farmers and their families than a good apple and peach orchard just coming into bearing. The purchaser in this can see at once the interest on his mortgage if purchased on a credit, as nine-tenths of farms are, and if an orchard of considerable size, the entire principal too by the day of maturity. If you have such a farm for sale, or one more particularly wearing out or thin in soil and unsightly for selling, take my advice, plant an orchard, for it will be not only a benefit to you but a lasting advantage to your purchaser.

VARIETIES OF PEACHES FOR CULTIVATION.

From the great varieties of peaches recommended in the different peach growing districts of the country, selections have been made of such as have been found on trial as best adapted to the different localities.

In all such selections regard should be paid to those combining the elements of good marketable fruit, good keepers, healthy, large, fine color, and of vast importance, to be good carriers, standing safe transportation to market, and such as ripen in regular succession from the earliest to the latest, extending through the peach season from about the middle of July to the middle or last of October, in a region near the city of Philadelphia.

The following list contains the most of the leading varieties grown and fruited in the peach districts of Maryland, Delaware and Pennsylvania, and have for the most part been well adapted to the Eastern and Western States. Many of the kinds named have been standard varieties for the last thirty to fifty years and over, and have not been superceded in their good qualities as paying market fruits. Others have been introduced within a later period for superior excellence, such as Crawford's Late and early Reeves' Favorite, Mountain Rose, Stump the World, &c. We have now a class of new early peaches, mostly from the seed of the Hale's Early, that ripen in Pennsylvania in July. Among them are Alexander, Amsden's June, Downing, Early Beatrice. These and other varieties are offered by our nurserymen, and although they have not as yet been sufficiently tested, some of them offer well, and are worthy of early trial, as they commence the peach season nearly a month in advance of the Early York, which some thirty years back was about the first peach in the market, its season here in Pennsylvania being from about the fourth to the tenth of August. The Early Alexander was ripe here in 1879, from the 15th to the 23d of July. The Amsden's June and Downing are even earlier. It is to be hoped that they all may prove more valuable than their parent, "Hale's Early," which is now in Maryland and Delaware as well as in Pennsylvania, pretty generally supplanted by more reliable varieties. I feel hopeful that some of these new varieties will prove themselves entirely reliable.

Name.	Color.	Quality.	Ripe.
Amsden's June.	Red	Good	July.
Alexander	Red	Good.	July.
Downing	Red and White	Good.	July.
Wilder	Red and White	Good size	July.
Beatrice	Red and White	Small.	July.

THE PEACH

Name.	Color.	Quality.	Ripe.
Hale's Early	Red and White	Rots badly	Aug.
Troth's Early	Red and White	Fine Market Peach	Aug.
Mount'n Rose	Red and White	Good Market Peach	Aug.
Early York	Red and White	Popular.	Aug.
Crawf d's Early	Yellow	Large and Good	Aug.
Yellow Rare Ripe	Yellow	Large and Good	Aug.
Morris Favorite	Red and White	Large and Good	Aug.
Oldmixon	Red and White	Large and Fine	Aug.
Foster	Yellow	Like Crawford Early	Aug.
George IV	Yellow	Beautiful	Aug.
Reeves' Fav'te	Yellow	Large, Splendid	Sept.
Fox Seedling	Red and White	Excellent bearer	Sept.
Crawford's Late	Yellow	Splendid, Valuable	Sept.
Shipley's Red	Red and White	Valuable	Sept.
Grosse Mignone	Red and White	Fine peach	Sept.
Stump the World	Red and White	Very fine	Sept.
Susquehanna	Yellow	Very large	Sept.
Ward's Late, Free	Red and White	Popular	Sept.
Patterson's White	White	Very fine	Sept.
Crocket's Late White	White	Great bearer	Sept.
Free Heath	White	Good	Sept.
Free Smock	Yellow	Valuable	Oct.
Salway	Yellow		Oct.
Late Heath	White	Valuable	Oct.
Headly	Ripening after the Heath.		

EXTRACTS

From the Proceedings of the Pennsylvania Fruit Growers' Society, at its Twenty-first Annual Meeting, held at Bethlehem, Pa., January 21 and 22, 1880. Judge Stitzel, President, of Reading, Pa., in the Chair.

Mr. Thomas W. Harvey, of Chester County, Chairman of the Committee on Orcharding, reported with other interesting matter that Mr. John Rutter, of West Chester, had prepared an exhaustive paper on the Peach and its diseases, containing an experience of over thirty years in its culture in Chester and Delaware counties, Pennsylvania, and in the State of Maryland, showing that peaches can be more successfully grown and put into the markets in better condition and to much greater profit from these counties than from Delaware and Maryland, and he hoped that it would be asked for by the Society, whereupon Messrs. Harvey, Sattherwaite and Noble were appointed a committee to wait on Mr. Rutter and to invite him to give his experience and views to the Society on peach growing.

* * * * *

Mr. Josiah Hoopes said "the election of new members, he believed, is always in order, and the man I now propose to elect, twenty years ago, did more than any one in the organization and early prosperity of the Society, and he now moved that John Rutter, Esq., of West Chester, be elected an honorary member of this Society. Mr. Rutter was elected by acclamation.

* * * * *

The Committee on Mr. Rutter's paper on Peach Growing, reported that the paper referred to was a manuscript of a treatise on the culture of the Peach and its diseases, remedies, &c., just prepared for publication, that it was too voluminous for a single address, and recommended that extracts be read from it. The Secretary now read such extracts as were selected. They were lengthy and very exhaustive. These, with Mr. Rutter's very able address before the Society, presented clearly his mode of culture, treatment of the diseases of the Peach, &c.

He gave a brief history of the introduction of the peach into the American colonies, adaptability of our soil and climate to its growth, and great productiveness, continuing in health and vigor to an old age, affording annually its delicious tribute as a luxury to the early colonists. About the commencement of the American Revolution a change suddenly came over the health and productiveness of the tree, first appearing near Philadelphia, as reported by Judge Peters, Mr. Heston and other peach growers of that day, and this change they spoke of was that fatal disease the yellows. It has continued its ravages on the orchard with almost unremitted virulence ever since, and owing to the disease, peach growers were discouraged in extensive planting in Pennsylvania for market purposes. New Jersey, Delaware and Maryland became the peach growing regions to supply our markets, and for the last fifty years the two last named States have enjoyed an almost entire monopoly of the peach market in Philadelphia and New York. Mr. Rutter next treated of his successful system of peach growing for years in Chester and Delaware counties, both diseased districts and subject to the yellows, showing that under his treatment peaches were grown successfully, and more so than in the healthy districts in Southern Maryland, and with much greater profit to the producer. The yellows is a specific disease affecting the peach, and the cause assigned, and pretty generally now conceded, is a parasitic fungi, and the remedies are found in caustic alkalies. These remedies were elaborately and exhaustively treated. He gave a chemical analysis of the peach, apple and pear tree, showing that the three great and leading elements were lime, potash and phosphate of lime, and that the fertilizing elements required for one were the proper food for the others; that two of these three elements, lime and potash, which contributed so largely in their composition and healthful growth, were the very agents, when properly prepared and applied, that proved destructive to all the enemies of the tree, whether from insects or parasitic fungi. Quick or caustic lime, potash, guano and all the ammoniacal alkalies, act as purifiers and produce the desired result—the entire destruction of these diseases, whether in the body, limbs or roots of the tree; in the one case by the application of a wash, and to the roots a treatment of lime, which is preferred to ashes on account of its cheapness, convenience and access, and as favorably known to every farmer as an indispensible agent in the fertilizing of his soil. The peach tree, he said, is an improver of the soil, and lands of medium fertility are to be preferred for peach orchards, as the ground will continue to improve yearly under cultivation.

The peach is the least expensive crop on the farm; this brings peach growing within the capacity of all as a cheap, available and profitable crop. The successful growing of this delicious fruit is of the highest importance to every one, from the farmer with his broad acres and his thousands of trees, to the town, village and country housekeeper who has a yard or lawn, however limited. Each can become his own peach grower on a sufficient scale to supply with a few thrifty trees his entire wants in this delicious fruit. In a few short years the farmers of the six eastern counties of the State, Lancaster, Chester, Delaware, Montgomery, Bucks and Berks, within a few hours each of the market, will be found relieving us from our dependence on Delaware and Maryland, our two two neighboring States, which have enjoyed a monopoly of our city markets for the last fifty years.

The result of Mr. Rutter's peach growing in Pennsylvania and Maryland, on a large scale for a series of years—the first in a district diseased with the yellows, and the other in a healthy location not in any way affected with the disease—is information that is vastly to the advantage of Pennsylvania in quantity and quality of fruit. The uncertainty of the peach crop is increased as we leave Pennsylvania and proceed South, even into Georgia and Florida. Again, the fruit shipped from Maryland, he said, is gathered in an immature state, quite hard, and before it has acquired that sweet saccharine taste which is only found in a ripe peach. This immature condition is required for peaches handled so frequently and roughly in their long transportation. They ripen on their way to market and never attain the rich, luscious taste of a fully matured peach. The peach is perishable at maturity and requires a near market and careful handling. As to the profits in peach growing between the North and South—a distance of one hundred and fifty miles—there is no approximate comparison, Pennsylvania having so greatly the advantage of nearness of market and superior condition of fruit.

At the conclusion of Mr. Rutter's address, on motion of H. M. Engle, of Marietta, the following resolution was passed:

Resolved, That the hearty thanks of this Society are hereby tendered to Mr. John Rutter, of West Chester, for his generosity in giving us the benefit of his most valuable and long experience in peach culture.

INDEX.

Introduction,	3
General Remarks on the Peach,	5
First Appearance of the Yellows,	10
Treatment of Peach Farm near West Chester, Pa.	22
Difficulties to be Overcome,	29
Experience in Peach Growing in Maryland,	34
Location and Soil for Peach Culture,	38
Directions for Planting, etc.,	40
Advantages of Peach Culture,	47
Manures and Remedial Agents,	50
Benefits of Potash, etc.,	55
Quick Lime the Great Remedy,	59
Indications of Yellows in the Peach,	65
Peach Borer, etc.,	74
Pruning,	77
The Value of Peach Growing,	81
Varieties of Peaches for Cultivation,	86
Extracts from Proceedings of Fruit Growers' Convention,	89
Index,	95

MORRIS NURSERIES,

ESTABLISHED 1848

120 Acres in Cultivation,

GEO. ACHELIS,

PROPRIETOR,

West Chester, Pa.,

———:o:———

A LARGE ASSORTMENT OF

PEACH, APPLE, PEAR,

CHERRY TREES, ETC.,

ORNAMENTAL TREES AND SHRUBS,

EVERGREENS, IN GREAT VARIETY,

SMALL FRUITS, GRAPE VINES,

CLIMBING VINES, ROSES, ETC., ETC.,

Always on Hand.

———:o:———

Correspondence Solicited.

EVERY SATURDAY NIGHT.

A WEEKLY PAPER,

Published Every Saturday

IN

HARRISBURG, PA.

EDITED BY DR. J. R. HAYES.

And Devoted to
Literature, Science, Agriculture and Farming Interests in General,

Essays Upon the Proper Cultivation of Tobacco, published from time in this Journal,

Essays Upon the Use of Fertilizers and Method of Application.

EVERY SATURDAY NIGHT is a Live Family Newspaper, Full of Information for the Household, free from descriptions of Murders, Crimes, Etc.

Price, $2 per year, invariably in advance.

Send and get specimen copy

Address "Every Saturday Night," Harrisburg, Pa.

www.ingramcontent.com/pod-product-compliance
Lightning Source LLC
Chambersburg PA
CBHW031121160426
43192CB00008B/1068